1950 1951 1952 1953 1954 1955 1956 1957 1958 1959

THE 1950s was very much a transitional period for Arbroath and its people as they slowly recovered from the rigours and shortages of the Second World War which still loomed large in the collective memory. The new decade was perceived as a new opportunity, a time when things could - and would - only get better.
Year on year, the townsfolk carried on their daily lives, working hard towards a better life, enjoying the boom of cinematic entertainment in the three cinemas, The Olympia, The Picture House and The Palace, none of which remains today. Local talent came very much to the fore in the days when a television set was a luxury for only those who were very well off.
Arbroath Amateur Operatic Society continued its proud tradition of staging sell-out shows in the Webster Hall and Arbroath Amateur Dramatic Club grew from strength to strength.
The end of sugar rationing in 1953 was joyfully welcomed by children of all ages, and for the adults was an indicator that things were, indeed, getting back to normal following the uncertainties of the war years and their aftermath.
As local companies such as Frasers, Shanks, Keith Blackman, Leatherflor,

Reekies and many others responded to the needs of a growing world economy, the town's fishing fleet expanded and modernised to supply the populace with health-giving fish, and farmers, too, took advantage of the latest mechanical harvesters and other modern aids.
However, the community of St Tammas was dealt a major blow late in 1953 when the Arbroath lifeboat, RNLB 'Robert Lindsay', capsized at the entrance to the harbour on returning from a call-out and six of her seven-man crew perished. It was a tragedy that still haunts the people of Arbroath even now, 50 years on.
However, within a very short period of time another lifeboat was operating from the station, with a new crew, far more having volunteered their services than could ever be accommodated.
During this time, Arbroath's coastal trade regenerated, with cargo vessels arriving at the harbour with flax and timber, the main items of numerous commodities, and leaving again with, among other things, potatoes and barley.
As the 1960s approached, the town was caught up in the rock and roll phenomenon and the younger element in society began to make their thoughts more widely - and loudly - known.

Tearooms soon became cafes, and Coca-Cola was the drink of choice of those too young to indulge in anything stronger. The town prospered, tourism boomed, and as cars became more commonplace, caravan parks blossomed all over the place. Then, much too quickly the 1950s were gone. The Beatles and Stones were just months awa continued apace in bonnie A

BRIAN J. FORSYTH

Wir Bookie o' the 1950s, by Brian J. Forsyth. Published by Johnston (Falkirk) Ltd., Redbrae Road, Camelon, Falkirk, FK1 4ZA.

Scouts of 2nd Arbroath at a camp-fire in the Scout Huts in February, 1950. They are, from left, back - F. Millar, D. Cooper, Roger Shellard, W. Timms, W. Black, Harold Graham, Joe Addison, Scoutmaster; Ken Moir, Bruce Walker, Gus Petrie and David Jolly: front - Alastair Ogg, Stanley Bowen, A. Rattray, Bill Cowie, K. Herron, C. Batchelor, G. Reid, Ian Strachan and Douglas Crarer.

Mr Roland Ewing, a professional singer and later a teacher in Arbroath, with some of his pupils who comprised the Roland Ewing Concert Party, at a function in St Ninian's Church hall in 1950. Pictured are, from left, back row - Sheila Walker, Marie Scott, Nessie Baird, Pat Sweeney, Margaret Lowe and Alice Shepherd: second row - Richard Cargill, Lily McCaffrey, Bruce Walker, Sylvia Swankie, --------, Margaret Fox, Edward Buchan and Mr Ewing: third row - Agnes Stott, --------, Helen Spence, -- Stott, Ruth Spink, -------- and -- Stott: front row - Freda McGregor, Gladys McGregor and June Smith.

In January, 1950, the Arbroath fishing boat, 'Girl Jean', owned by Joe Cargill, was stolen from the harbour by a 14-year-old local youngster, John Guthrie, 27 Dishlandtown Street, prompting a massive air and sea search. The vessel was discovered after three days by the Hull trawler, 'Reptonian', 165 miles due east of Arbroath. She was returned to Arbroath after being absent for a week and our picture shows the vessel being examined for damage shortly after berthing near the dock gates. At the stern is Alex Gerrard, of Gerrard Bros., boatbuilders, and those at the bow are, from left - Rob Cargill, Dave Beattie, John Cargill, Joe Cargill, skipper; and Sid Cargill.

A forgotten corner of Arbroath under a blanket of snow in February, 1950. The main building is Arbroath Auction Mart - 'the Mert' - in Park Street at the junction with Millgate, and extending through to Panmure Street. It closed at the end of 1967 and was demolished shortly thereafter. The former Alma Mill, now converted to housing, can be seen just beyond the corner of the Arbroath Herald building, at left. The picture was taken from the doorway of Brothockbank House.

Principals in Arbroath Musical Society's production of 'The Desert Song' which received rave reviews during its week-long run in the Webster Memorial Hall in February, 1950. They are, from left, back - A.M.L. Rae, C.C. McDonald, A.W. Brown, John Corbett, Alan Wilkie, George Morris, Ian Spalding, R.B. Brown and R. Somerville: front - Jack Lamb, Cissie Fleming, Marjory Dutch, Pricilla Ritchie and Elizabeth Logie.

Arbroath Half-Holiday FC during the 1949/50 season. They are, from left, back - Teel Becci, George Chalmers, Eddie Forbes, Willie Munro, Bill Ritchie, Jack Ironside, Jim Tosh and Len Herron: front - Jackie Robb, George McKenzie, Arthur Carrie, Jackie Christison and Peter Cant.

The Abbey School primaries four and five choir which competed in the Arbroath Musical Festival in 1950. It comprised, from left, back row - --------, Marjory Fox, --------, Sandy Steele, Atholl Robertson and Irene Gordon: third row - Gena Dickson, Agnes Hadden, Charlie Borland, Elizabeth Spink, Wilma Peters, Maureen Buchan, Margaret Tasker, Norma Donaldson and Jessie Beattie: second row - James Croall, Vera Bridges, June Gemmell, Isobel Ritchie, Wilma Cargill, Lillian Stewart and Ronnie Crichton: front row - Sandy Milne, Ronnie Campbell and John Bowen.

A distinctive part of old Arbroath that disappeared in the redevelopment in Guthrie Port in the mid-1960s. Ron Brown's general, fruit, vegetables, flowers and gardening shop at 61 to 65 Guthrie Port as it was probably about 1950. Note the message bike at the front door, for the proclaimed delivery service, and the many wall-mounted vending machines, a feature never seen on outdoor locations nowadays.

A tranquil summer evening at Arbroath Harbour probably in 1950. The vessel entering harbour is the 'Girl Jean', skippered by Joe Cargill, 2 Shore, and that lying nearest as the 'Restless Wave', skippered by Peter Smith, 7 Old Shore Head. The huddle of people round the lamp-post are local fish merchants bidding for the catch just landed.

Previous page - Arbroath Town Missionary, Mr Robert Clapham, marked his golden jubilee with a marvellous party in the ultra-modern Arbroath Mission Centre in July of the millennium year, 2000. Our picture dates back to his early days in post, surrounded by local youngsters during the winter of 1950. Can you spot yourself?

Right - An extension to the Helen Street clubrooms of the Arbroath and district branch of the British Legion was opened on Saturday, September 9, 1950, by Major General Douglas N. Wimberley, principal of University College, Dundee. Brigadier James A. Oliver, chairman, presided. Our picture shows Mr Tom Mann throwing the first bowl in the carpet bowling alley which was a feature of the new facility. Seen in the front row are, from left - G. Kerr, General Wimberley, S.H. Wallace, G. Cuthill, Sandy Christie, Harry Swankie and Brigadier Oliver. Among those in the background are William B. McDonald, vice-president; Provost Sir William Chapel, branch president; and Norman Fraser, vice-president.

Ashdale Football Club in the 1950/51 season. Pictured are, from left, back - Jimmy Jamieson, Tom Phillips, Willie Lawrie, Bill Fenton, Jim Knowles, Jake Ironside, John Currie, Andy Duncan, Andrew Duncan and Harry Gall: front - Dave Barclay, Jim Wilkie, Alec Paton, Willie Munro, Willie Nicoll, Jim Bowren, Ray Hayes and mascot, Atholl Robertson.

This picture of Arbroath Sea Rangers and friends dates from February, 1951, and was taken at a dance in either the Sea Cadet Hall, Arrott Street, or St Ninian's Church hall, held to raise funds for a subsequent trip to Switzerland. Pictured are, from left, back - Sandy Thomson, Wynne Addison, Ron Wilson, May Smith, Bill Ramsay, Jack Garden, Frank Garden, Bill Ramsay, Bob Crichton, Danny Fenton, Jack Black and Doug Paterson: front - Jean Edwards, Evelyn Petrie, Brenda Swankie, Miss Marie Black, Tarriebank, group leader; Irene Gillespie, Eva Robertson, Margaret McNab and Lexie Foster.

The beautiful ladies of 18th century New Orleans who appeared in Arbroath Amateur Operatic Society's presentation of 'New Moon' staged in the Webster Hall in February, 1951. They are, from left, back row - Mrs C. Hebenton, Mrs A.J.B. Hogg, Mrs Cissie Fleming and Ada Spink: middle row - Vera McLean, Mrs Marjory Dutch, Liza Suttie, Joan Mitchell, Audrey Gunn, Miss A. Pert, Miss M. Robb, Mrs G.H. Rodger, Miss F. Malcolm and Jean Birse: front row - Grace Allan, Miss J., Buick, Belle Smith, Joyce Duncan, Ada Butchart, Helen Colston and Miss W. Addison.

Their dashing male counterparts were, from left, back - Sandy Pert, G. Hutton, Terence Myles, George Bisset, Jim Osborough, G.S. Morris, John Murrison, J. Gordon Cronshaw, David Esplin and Murray Kinnear: front - A.W. Brown, George Rodger, John Blair, Ross Hunter, Murray Wallace, Gordon Smith and Jack Lamb.

The central feature of this aerial picture from 1951 is instantly recognisable to Arbroathians far and wide as the Round O, or St Catherine's Window, at Arbroath Abbey. In contrast to the rest of the picture, the Abbey has changed not at all in the intervening years. At bottom left is a corner of the Wyndies, featuring Greenbank, all of which has gone. In the centre is St Andrew's Church and at bottom right is Guthrie Port, the face of which has changed greatly. At top left can be seen one of the town's gasometers and just in front are the houses in Stanley Street which were demolished to make way for car parking at the beginning of 2002. In front of that is Abbey School, now replaced by Abbey Health Centre, and Abbey Church, now the Old and Abbey. At the other side of the street, at the top of Abbey Path, is the former foundry of Keith Blackman Ltd., fan engineers, which made way for a High Street redevelopment and car parking.

The *Arbroath Herald* was first on the scene to photograph the Stone of Destiny when it was returned to Arbroath Abbey on April 11, 1951, three months after its disappearance from Westminster Abbey. This picture, taken by *Herald* reporter, Arthur Binnie, shortly after the Stone's arrival shows, from left - Councillor D.A. Gardner, Mr George B. Lowe, Councillor Frank W.A. Thornton, James Wishart, Abbey custodian; Miss Violet Cobb, Miss Margaret Brodie, editor, *Arbroath Herald*; and Mr George S. Shepherd, assistant editor.

R.N.L.B. ROBERT LINDSAY

Left - On June 23, 1951, the Dowager Countess of Dalhousie named Arbroath's new lifeboat 'RNLB Robert Lindsday' at an impressive ceremony at the inner dock. The distinguished company of guests in attendance included the Duke of Montrose, Lady Chapel and the Hon Mrs Lindsay-Carnegie, Kinblethmont. Our picture shows the vessel colourfully dressed for the occasion. The crew members are, from left, in the bow - William Swankie, Charlie Smith and Rob Cargill; and at the stern - Harry Swankie, engineer; Dave Bruce, second coxswain; William Swankie snr., coxswain; and John Smith.

Right - Mary Adelaide, the Dowager Countess of Dalhousie, and the Duke of Montrose following the launch of RNLB 'Robert Lindsay'. The Dowager Countess was presented with a bouquet of flowers by Margaret Swankie.

How a grocery store looked in days gone by. Pictured amid what now might be considered a frenetic clutter of jars, tins, packets and fruit is Jimmy Robb in the store of John M. Dick at 249 High Street about 1951.

Members of St Ninian's Church Youth Fellowship record a play in the session house in May, 1951. They are, from left, standing - Ken Meekison, Alec Greenhowe, Barry Patterson, Earl Matthew, Ian Barclay, Ian Ross, Stewart Williamson, J. Colville, jnr. and the Rev Colin T. Day: front - J. Colville, Kathleen Norrie, Helen McNab, Valerie Colville, Margaret McNab and Irene Gair.

Arbroath Westburn FC pictured at Brechin prior to a Dundee and Angus Junior League match against Brechin Vics in 1951. They are, from left, back - Jimmy Lindsay, manager; Jack Wicks, Tommy Pearson, Ally Duncan, Jimmy Angus, Peem White, Fred Smith, Andy Hynd, senior, committee member; and Jim Middleton, committee: front - Stan Beattie, Jock Glen, Dave (Skip) Milne, Dave Dinnie, Andy Hynd, junior, and Alfie Wood, hamper boy.

Well-known Scottish dramatist and broadcaster, Mr Robert Kemp, accepted an invitation to open St Ninian's Church winter fair and sale of work held in the church hall, Brothock Bridge, in November, 1951. He is seen here with organisers of the event. Pictured are, from left - Mrs J. Arthur, Mr A. Christison, Mrs Day, Mr Kemp, Miss Ella Miller and the Rev Colin T. Day. In front is David Brown.

A scene at the High Altar of Arbroath Abbey from the Abbey Pageant of 1951. George S. Shepherd is Bernard de Linton, Lord Abbot of Aberbrothock, wearing a replica of the Monymusk Reliquary. Beside him are the Bishops of Dunkeld, Aberdeen and St Andrews, played by Tom Mathieson, D.L. Gardner, and David Goodwillie respectively and in the central window is co-producer, Frank W.A. Thornton, who was also commentator. Also pictured are standard-bearers, Barons, Canons and Monks following the re-enactment of the historic occasion.

Miss Mary Talbert (seated centre) who took the title role in Arbroath Amateur Operatic Society's production of 'No! No! Nanette' in the Webster Hall in February, 1952, pictured with the other leading players. They are, from left, back - Jack Lamb, Audrey Gunn, Ian Spalding, Elizabeth Bisset and Allan Wilkie: front - Elma MacFarlane, Mary Winton, Marjory Dutch and Cissie Fleming.

Boys of the 2nd Arbroath Scout who won the campfire class at Arbroath and District Musical Festival in March, 1952. They are, from left, back row - Ken Moir, Fred Millar, Alistair Ogg, Harold Graham, Dave Jolly: middle row - Bobby Connell, Bill Cowie, George Fyfe, Ian Strachan, Jim Bowman, Stephen Myles: front row - Jack Campbell, Alan Strachan, Ian Craig, Doug McDonald, Alastair McSkimming, Harry McGeachie, Walter Strachan, Norman Millar and Joe Addison.

A peaceful early evening fishmarket on the harbour quayside in 1952. The large building at extreme right is the Commercial Inn, Old Shorehead. The council block adjacent to the slipway bridge was demolished in the late 1980s and the ground is now part of the boatyard.

Boys of Panther Patrol, 2nd Arbroath Scouts, pictured at their annual summer camp at West Migvie, Glenesk, in July 1952. Ready for inspection outside their tent are, from left - Fred Millar, Bobbie Connell, Ramsay Strachan, Alastair McSkimming and Ken Moir.

Arbroath High School pupils who enjoyed a school trip to Belgium in 1952 pictured during a visit to the beautiful city of Bruges. They are, from left, back row - Ian Nelson, --------, Lorna Murray, Wendy Chisholm, Ruth Anderson, Vera McColl: second row - Miss Riddle, --------; third row - Freda Ferguson, Elizabeth Smart, Margaret Smith, Helen Ferguson, Christian Esplin, Moyra Deuchar, Ella Cooper, --------, Norma Chisholm, Alistair Macdonald: fourth row - --------, Margaret Brown, Graham Reid, Dick Myers, --------, Ian Henderson: fifth row - Wendy Hennessy, --------, Alice Shepherd, Elizabeth Salmond, Doreen Anderson, Constance Grosset, Wilma Reid, Sandy Tapley, Bob Black, Ian Saunders, Bert Smart, Dick Calder, Alistair Ramsay: sixth row - Eleanor Boyle, Ian Grant, Cora Fleming: seventh row - Irene Grassie, Kathleen Forbes, June Meston, --------, --------, Kay Gardener, Johnny Foster, D.A. Gardener, Sandra Massie, Douglas Nairn, --------, Elspeth Nicol, Marion Fairfield, Ruth Samuel, --------: front row - Johnny Steven, Maureen Munro, Ronald Kidd, Colin McNab, Gordon Laird, Douglas Hamilton, --------, Muriel Thompson and Lorna Wilson. The gentlemen on either side were local guides.

On Saturday, August 15, 1952, Arbroath fishing boats, dressed with bunting and flags and laden with passengers, left the harbour and, led by the lifeboat, RNLB 'Robert Lindsay', cruised to the Ness as part of the general celebration in the town which accompanied that year's Arbroath Abbey Pageant. The popularity of the trips is evident from the number of people crammed on the decks of the vessels which are, in front, AH37, 'June Rose', owned and skippered by Bill Smith, 26 Ladybridge Street, and AH 76, 'Girl Jean', owned and skippered by Joe Cargill, 2 Shore.

Bishops lead this section of the Abbey Pageant cast past Tower Neuk and into High Street in August, 1952. The cast members were followed by a procession of historical tableaux on lorries, which had been prepared and entered by local firms and organisations. As the parade passed the town house, it was reviewed from a platform by Provost J.K. Moir and visiting dignitaries.

The setting was the Imperial Hotel in 1952 and the occasion was the annual smoker of Arbroath Boating Club. As well as members of the local club, the picture includes guests from Dundee Corinthians Boating Club. Pictured are, from left, back row - David Duke, Jim Anderson and Norman Robb: middle row - Tom Crow, Dave Simpson, Norman Smith, Davie Mill, --------, Will Carrie, Chick Ferrier, Fred Ohren, Davie Crabbe, Jim Kydd, Jock Walker, Ally Brown and Bert Nicol: front row - Dave Matthew, --------, --------, Tam Swankie, Mick Robb, --------, --------, -------- and Alec Pert.

In September, 1952, Arbroath Town Council agreed to make representations to the National Trust to request that Newgate House, the last mansion house of its kind in Arbroath, be preserved, perhaps as a folk museum and cultural centre. The exact date of construction of the house is unknown, but it was probably built during the 17th century and in the latter half of that century was occupied by Robert Carnegie of Newgate and his family. Towards the end of the 18th century, the estate of Newgate was in the possession of a family by the name of Butchart. At that time, Newgate House, set in the midst of an orchard and surrounded by cornfields, was a delightful country house. Newgate Bowling Green is laid out on part of the garden of the old mansion house. The house was acquired by Angus Housing Association and was restored in the late 1970s with financial help from Angus District Council and the Historic Buildings Council for Scotland. It was reopened in October, 1980, by Peter Fraser MP.

The cast of Arbroath Amateur Dramatic Club's presentation of Kenneth Horne's comedy 'Fools Rush In' staged in the Webster Hall in October, 1952. Pictured are, from left, back - Ian Spalding, Shena Middleton, Dick Manders, Jeanette Whiter, Margaret Swankie and Dorothy Stevenson: front - Gwen Williams and George S. Shepherd.

This evening picture of Arbroath High Street was taken on December 19, 1952. The deserted thoroughfare, with many of the shop windows still lit, gives an ethereal impression of the town's major shopping centre. Although many of the businesses have changed in the intervening years, the buildings have hardly altered at all, with only the shopfronts having been restyled. In the centre of the picture can be picked out the two decorated street lights which stood outside the Town House, now Arbroath Sheriff Court.

Employees of A. Nicol and Co's Chalmers Street works pictured at their Christmas party in the Windmill Hotel in December, 1952. They are, from left, standing - --------, --------, Mary Coutts, Lizzie Clark, Nobby Clark, Kathleen Ramsay, --------, Sam Shepherd, Belle Gunning, -------, Bill Gunning, --------, --------, Danny Cargill, Betty Leuchars, Marina Walker, Winnie Addison, June Walker, Jim Gibb, Effie Scrimgeour, Jim Fairweather, Jean Rennie and Walter Kerr: seated - Sheila Pratt, Win Cargill, Vi Gray, --------, Belle Addison, Jean Boath, --------, Jean Cargill, Margaret Fleming, Margaret Smith, --------, Mary Shepherd, --------, Frank Smith, Margaret Swankie, Bella Culbert, Johnny Scrimgeour, Evelyn Gibb, --------, --------, Vi Smith, Marie Rae, Donald Smith, --------, Margaret Reid, Martha Mowatt and Nan Stirling.

Miss Jean Ferrier and Miss Sheila Silver, proprietors of the North Sea Hotel, with friends and staff at a party on January 30, 1953. Pictured are, from left, back row - Bill McFarlane, Yvonne Thomson, -- McBey, Annie Soutar, -- McBey, Jim Chapman, Peter Cowie, Dave Wylie, Ada Stewart, Donald McLean, Ann Clark McLean, Jim Fyfe, Mrs Fyfe, Belle Cadman, Alex Cargill, George Shepherd, Mrs Wylie, Mrs Saunders, John Thomson and Mrs Miller: middle row - Winnie Thomson, Mary Robertson, ------, Jean Ferrier, Sheila Silver, ------, Mrs Oswald and Mrs Robertson: front row - -- Oswald, ------, -- Miller, Bill Campbell, Bert Soutar and Gerald Silver.

Houses in Arbroath were hard hit during a spectacular storm which raged on the last day of January, 1953. Thousands of pounds worth of damage was caused in and around the town by the gales, described as the worst in living memory. A milkman and a message boy were cut by falling debris but, mercifully, no-one was seriously injured. A hole was torn in the roof of the house at 20 St Mary Street, occupied by 93-year-old Mrs Margaret G. Halkett, and the public baths in Marketgate were evacuated by the superintendent, Mr William Dakers, who feared that the roof might collapse. Leonard Street, Sidney Street, Airlie Crescent and Strathmore Avenue had a wartime look with debris from blown-down chimney heads and lifted slates strewn all over the place. Our picture shows Sidney Street at 2 o'clock on the afternoon of the storm.

In March, 1953, Arbroath Instrumental Band, under bandmaster Jack Boyle, gave their first concert in the Webster Memorial Hall for some years and they had for the occasion new uniforms of navy blue, scarlet and gold. The concert drew a large audience and featured soloists, Miss Elizabeth Dall, the well-known Arbroath-born singer, and Mr Conway Stuart, tenor, who was making his first concert appearance in his adopted home town. Miss Isobel Nekola was Miss Dall's accompanist and Mrs Nan McLeod accompanied Mr Stuart. The concert was arranged by Provost J. K. Moir and Miss Patricia Hutchison presented Miss Dall with a bouquet. The longest serving member taking part was Mr John McEwan, who had been a bandsman since the formation of the band in 1893. Our picture of the band and guests shows, from left, back row - Fergus Lundie, James Crowe, Alex Petrie, Vic Lewis, James Williamson, Tom Peebles, Cyril Spurway and Ernie Gerrard: middle row - William Boyle, Alistair Crowe, Bill Jarrett, Don Williamson, Ron Petrie, George Grant, Jack McEwan and Ian Cargill: front row - Fred Mosley, Morris Taylor, Jack Boyle, Nan McLeod, Isobel Nekola, Betty Dall, Conway Stuart, Provost Moir, Patricia Hutchison, Fred Crowe and Willie Jarrett.

On Sunday, May 30, 1953, a Cross of Sacrifice was unveiled in a moving ceremony in the Western Ceremony. Constructed of white stone, the memorial was erected by the Imperial War Graves Commission in memory of the 73 personnel who died while serving at HMS Condor and HMS Peewit, at Easthaven. The service was conducted by the Rev. Angus Loggan, Old Parish Church, and an introduction was read by Provost J.K. Moir. The dedication was conducted by the Rev J.K. Boulton Jones, senior chaplain, HMS Condor. Also present were Vice-Admiral E.M.C. Abel-Smith, RN, first commanding officer at Condor, and the Rev Carndoc Hughes, RN, HMS Condor. Praise was led by Arbroath Instrumental Band and an augmented choir from Arbroath churches.

Arbroathians of all age groups, in common with people from all corners of the UK and far-flung reaches of the British Empire, on June 2, 1953, celebrated the Coronation of Queen Elizabeth by gaily decorating their houses with bunting and flags, organising street parties, and giving gifts. This picture shows some of those, mainly resident in Green Street, who attended a party in the rooms of Lodge St Vigean (No 101). Bailie Eric B. Mackintosh and Mrs Mackintosh (right of centre) attended the event and handed out gifts of coronation mugs, pencil cases and sweets. Included in the picture are, back - Mrs McSkimming, Mrs Maxwell, Clara Mitchell, Sheila Geddes, Bill Strachan, Elizabeth Rennie, Marlene Bogue, George Murray, Audrey Russell, Olive Kennedy. Violet Bogue, Donald Mathieson, Eddie Maxwell, Mrs Kinnear, Lewis Kinnear, Doris Murray, Loraine Fitchet, Mary Carini, Winnie Carini, Walter Bogue, ---- Murray, Mrs McGregor, jnr., Dave Strachan, George McSkimming, Mrs McGregor, Allan McSkimming, Annie McGregor, Mrs Mackintosh, Mrs Gert Strachan, Donald Mathieson, Mrs Jessie Smith, Sy Smith, Bailie Mackintosh, Mac Strachan, David Kydd, Stewart Christie jnr., Alistair McSkimming, Charlie Mathieson, Tom Bogue, Bobby Connell: front - Moira McGregor, Margaret Christie, Jenny McGregor, Rena McGregor, Ada Rennie, Michael ------, Jean Rennie, Michael Kucharski, Maureen Maxwell, Sylvia Murray, Veronica Carini, Joyce Gibb, Evelyn Bogue, Sandra Smith, who presented a bouquet of flowers to Mrs Mackintosh; Sandra Auchterlony, Pam Auchterlony and, at the end of the row, Irene McKenzie.

The Coronation in Westminster Abbey on June 2, 1953, of Her Majesty Queen Elizabeth caused great excitement throughout the country and in Arbroath, Red Lichties went to great lengths to make public their joy. This picture shows the bonnie sandstone houses in Green Street which, some three decades later, were demolished to make way for development.

The way it was! Happy youngsters frolic by the fountain at Arbroath's outdoor bathing pool in midsummer, 1953. Although it appears to have been raining, the children play on totally unconcerned by the vagaries of the weather.

A crowd of over 6,000 spectators, comprising visitors and locals alike, assembled at Victoria Park on Saturday, July 11, 1953, for the open-air entertainment organised by Arbroath Publicity Council. Heavy rain meant that portions of the programme had to be curtailed, but the spectators were enthralled by the daredevil antics of Aerienne du Svede who performed at the top of a 100 foot tower despite driving rain and high winds. Eddie Najling and Wally Lanceley received a standing ovation when they returned to terra firma after their breathtaking performance.

The very first Miss Arbroath beauty competition to be held under the aegis of Arbroath Publicity Council took place at Arbroath's world famous outdoor swimming pool in the early part of July, 1953. It was won by 15-year-old shorthand typist, Robina Pollock, from Hardgate, Clydebank, with Barbara Bonar (17), Bishopbriggs, Glasgow, in second place and Margaret Niven, 5 Culloden Crescent, Arbroath, third. Our picture shows the contestants about to set off on their customary trip round the pool, marshalled by Mr J. Laurie Robertson, Publicity Council secretary, and Mr Neil Gow, entertainments manager.

The primary one intake at Arbroath High School in 1953. Pictured are, from left, back row - Jeffrey Dugdale, --------, David Gove, David Scott, David Thornton, Morris Pert and Ian Yule: second row - David Lackie, Graeme Morrison, Roderick McLean, Ian Begg, Clause Yule, --------, Neil Forrester, Colin Armstrong, Ralph Skea and David Smith: third row - Clive Rubens, David Brewster, John Milne, Nancy Goodwillie, Linda McGregor, Linda Millar, Calerie Thornton, Ronald Duncan, Alex Cargill and Keith Ruxton: front row - Monica Page, Barbara Lockhart, Honor Riley, Louise Hogben, Frances Ritchie, Lesley Rae, Carolyn Anderson, Jean Anderson, Marjory Morton, Pat Snowden, Mary Lowe and Wendy Dale.

The Earl of Southesk performed the opening ceremony at Inverbrothock Church bazaar in the Drill Hall, now the Community Centre, Marketgate, in August, 1953. Others in the group are Mr Henry Hood, Mrs Dutch, the Rev J. H. Dutch, and Mr E.J. Joss with, in front, Douglas Kydd and Anne Blyth, both of whom presented gifts to Lord Southesk.

How many Arbroathians heading toward retirement will remember this occasion. Taken in the Palace Cinema, James Street, in 1953, Lady Provost Mrs Jessie Mitchell is seen presenting prizes to winners of a competition for young cowboys, cowgirls and Indians at the ABC Minors' matinee. The other adults in the picture are Mr H.E. (Eddie) George, manager, and Mrs Hannah, secretary.

On October 18, 1953, Inverbrothock Parish Church, James Street, celebrated its 125th anniversary with special services attended by over 1200 people. The Rev John A. Fraser, Hamilton, a chaplain to Her Majesty The Queen, preached the sermons at both the morning and evening services, assisting the minister, the Rev John Henry Dutch. Later in the week, the church's new halls were dedicated by another Queen's chaplain, the Rev T.B. Stewart Thomson, Dunbarney, Perthshire. Our commemorative picture features, from left, back row - David McKenzie, Jack Lowe, John Gordon, George Edgar, George Anderson, Dave Dunbar, George Kydd, William Farquhar, Andrew W. Halliday, Robert Chapman, John Verth, William Anderson, John Gordon, Alec Grimmond and Sid Crammond: middle row - J. Kerr, George Sanderson, Alf Anderson, William Robb, Tom Hill, Dave Hutton, William Coutts, Henry Hood, John Miller, G. Donaldson, A.C. Patterson, Jim Donald, James Oram, Edward Dutch, William Kydd, James McGregor, F.W. Ferguson and James Hood: front row - Ed Dunbar, J.P. MacFarlane, John F. Webster, Edward J. Joss, Pat Robb, the Rev John A. Fraser, the Rev John Henry Dutch, Alex Miller, David Denholm, James Craig, James Edwards and George Stephen.

Six members of the crew of the Arbroath lifeboat - David Bruce, coxswain; Harry Swankie, mechanic; and crewmen William Swankie, Tom Adams, David Cargill and Charles Cargill - were tragically lost in gale-force conditions on Tuesday, October 27, 1953 when the 'Robert Lindsay' overturned at the entrance to Arbroath Harbour in the early hours of the morning. This is the terrible sight that was revealed as dawn broke. The lifeboat had been called out by the Coastguards at Fife Ness, along with the Anstruther Lifeboat, after distress rockets had been seen by the Coastguards. The weather was dreadful, and the Anstruther boat almost failed to make it out of its home harbour. The area where the flares had been seen was searched, but nothing was found, and the boats set off for their home ports at about 4.30 a.m. Coxswain Bruce, had been advised by Forth Coastguards to lie off the harbour until daylight. The lifeboat cruised offshore, but witnesses were aghast as its lights suddenly disappeared when the boat was hit by a cross wave, the result of the south-east gale creating mountainous seas on the bar at the harbour entrance. There was only one survivor, Archie Smith, the second coxswain, who was miraculously rescued when he caught a line, fired in the direction of voices crying for help in the pitch blackness. A funeral service was held for the six at the Old Church on the Saturday, and a solemn procession, led by the Lord Lieutenant of the County of Angus, the Earl of Airlie; and the Deputy Lieutenant, Brigadier J.A. Oliver, walked the mile-long route to the Eastern Cemetery, through driving rain. An estimated 10,000 people lined the route.

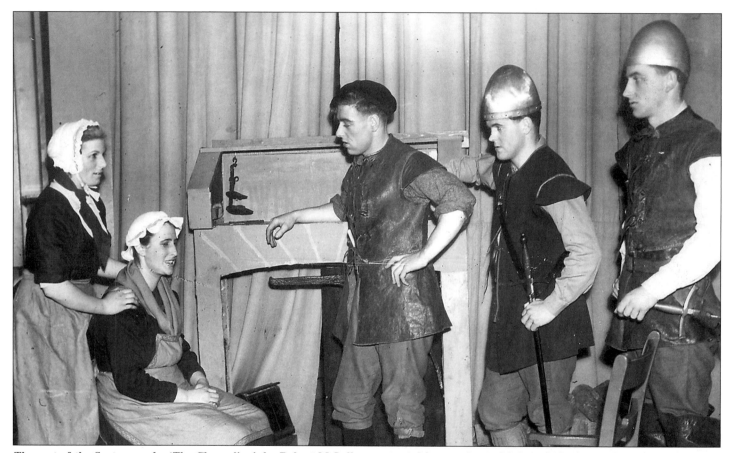

The cast of the Scots comedy, 'The Changeling', by Robert McLellan, presented by members of Arbroath Junior Agricultural Club in the Webster Theatre in January, 1954, as their entry in a drama festival run by the Angus Association of JACs. Pictured are, from left - Joyce Soutar, Templeton; May Stirling, Dickmontlaw; Hugh Robertson, Seaton of Auchmithie; Dave Smith, Poole Farm; and John Goodfellow, East Newton. Also taking part was Margaret Crockatt and the show was produced by Mr James B. Crockatt, Peebles Farm. The Arbroath club won the competition and went forward to the Eastern area final held in Perth High School where they also won, beating Central Fife JAC and Blairgowrie and district JAC.

Principals of Arbroath Amateur Operatic Society's production of 'Showboat' which ran in the Webster Memorial Theatre from Monday, February 1, to Saturday, February 6, 1954. They are, from left, back - Wilfred E. Forrester, Audrey Gunn, Ian Spalding, Margaret Robb, Andrew Keith and J.W.R. Lamb: front - Mary Talbert, Cissie Fleming and Marjory Cumming.

Fish salesman, Sid Crammond (with hat) makes a point to local merchant, George Beattie, during a quayside sale in March, 1954. Also in the crowd are Peter Pert, Alex Cargill, John Smith, Bob Spink, Betts Swankie, Tom Cargill and Nell Heenan.

During the 1953-54 season, Arbroath Lads' Club enjoyed considerable success in many league fixtures culminating in the under-18s and under-16s teams winning no fewer than four trophies. The Under-l8 League Cup, the Keith Cup and the Henderson Rosebowl were won by the under-18s team, and the Supplementary League Cup was won by the under-16s squad. In our picture are the club officials and the players who brought the honours to Arbroath, having beaten opponents from throughout Angus and Dundee. They are, from left, back row - Ed Fuyre, Dave Smith, Bob Smith, Vic Ritchie, Jocky Petrie, captain; Ian Chrystal, Billy Shepherd, Frank McEwan, Bert Smart, Jim Fairweather, Eddie Gray, Jimmy Smith and Willie Robb, president; middle row - Bert Herron, coach; Dave Easson, secretary; Jock Jolly, Jim Kennedy, Ron Crichton, Jake Watt, Roy Matthews, captain; Ian Mathews, Jimmy Walker, Gordon Stewart, Myles Cowie, Bill Jarret, David Air, Sandy Christie, Charlie Spink, vice-president; and Chick Mathieson; front row - Willie Marr, John Bryce, Willie Edmonds, Allan Kennedy, Billy Milne, John Murray, Jim Robb, John Middleton, Neil Hosie, Alec Milne, captain; and Stan Matthew; at front - Brian Esplin and Jack McFarlane.

In April and May, 1954, Arbroath Harbour enjoyed a sustained boom period, its busiest since before the Second World War, when an average of four boats per week berthed to take on cargoes of grain. They were running a shuttle service to various ports in Denmark. The harbour also welcomed the first German freighter since 1939, the Adler, of Cologne, berthed at the far pier in the picture above. The photograph marked a unique occasion, with three vessels taking on grain at the same time. The other two are the Cromarty Firth, from Newcastle, at left, and the Gannochy, registered at Dundee, in the foreground. The week after the picture was taken, no fewer than six boats embarked grain at Arbroath.

The first meeting of cast members prior to the 1954 Arbroath Abbey Pageant took place in May of that year at the Abbey. Pictured are, from left - Ruby Melvin, C.J. Henny, Bob Meekison, George S. Shepherd, producer; Bill Shaw, George Greig, Ken Meekison, Alasdair Ogg, James Wishart, Abbey custodian; and Tom Mathieson.

Dating from July, 1954, this shot of Arbroath Harbour shows various local fishing boats lined up prior to taking holidaymakers out to sea for a trip. The boats, which are 'dressed overall' with flags and bunting, are, from left - AH 50, 'Sparkling Star', Alec Spink: AH 216, 'Golden Rule II', Chae and George Smith; AH 65, 'Sunshine', Eck Dinnie; and AH 22, 'Amber Queen', Alex Shepherd. Berthed at the far quay is AH 11, 'Annie Smith', John Smith.

A bazaar organised by St Vigeans and Auchmithie Churches and held in the Drill Hall, Marketgate, on July 10, 1954, was opened by the Right Honourable the Earl of Airlie, KT. Our picture shows the platform party which comprised, from left - the Hon. Mrs Lindsay Carnegie, Kinblethmont; the Rev. C.E. Duff, Eileen Grant, who presented Lord Airlie with a box of Arbroath Smokies and lobsters; Lord Airlie, Mrs Duff and Mr George W. Dunn. The event realised £1,017 towards the cost of a new heating system for St Vigeans Church.

There was a huge turnout when over 5,000 spectators arrived at Victoria Park on Saturday, July 17, 1954, for a Grass Track Motor Cycle meeting which attracted crack riders from all over the country. The event was sponsored by Arbroath Publicity Council and organised by Arbroath Motor Club. It featured prize money totalling £114, a substantial sum at that time, when a tradesman's pay would have been between £5 and £10 per week. Top riders on the day included Jimmy Coghlan, known as 'the Bankfoot Flash, Strathmore Sporting Club; Bob Grant, Perth Club; and Chic Robertson, Dunfermline Club.

Autumn holidaymakers visiting Arbroath at the end of September, 1954, mingled with interested locals as the dock gates, which had been in continuous use for 20 years, were removed to the slipway for examination and repair. As illustrated here, one of the gates, which weighed 15 tons each, was removed with the assistance of a crane from HMS Condor. The other was tilted by pulley-tackle and floated off on the afternoon tide.

A group of stalwarts of Arbroath Artisan Golf Club and their guests from Monifieth Golf Club taking a break from the rigours of competition during a match at Elliot in 1954. The group includes some weel-kent faces and comprises, from left, back row - Cameron Watt, Stewart Duff, Harry Reid, Bob Smith, Fred Lawrence, --------, David Fairweather, --------, Alastair Milne, Harry Beck, David Laird, --------, --------, Willie Bullock, --------, --------, David Smart, Alastair Fraser and Bill Meek: middle row - --------, Bill Smyth, Alex Grimmond, Andrew Blissett and Jack Wyllie: front row - Willie Robertson, Ron Skea, Ernie Faulkner, Arthur Esplin, Gordon Rae, Tom Reid, --------, Archie White, Walter Scott, --------, George Watt, Tom Leddie, -------- and --------.

Prizewinners in a talent competition organised by Mr H.E. (Eddie) George (extreme left), manager of the Palace Cinema, James Street, pictured with the judges, Mr George B. Lowe, Lady Provost Mrs A.B. Mitchell and Lieutenant Commander Rice, HMS Condor. First prize was won by 'The Hillbillies', comprising George Muir, Frank Milne, and James Hood. Miss Helen Watson was second and third place was shared by Miss Pat Sweeney and Mr James Birse.

A heavy fall of snow during February, 1955, gave the already picturesque village of Arbirlot a Christmas card appearance.

A view, on a chill February morning in 1955, of Glover Street, one of the little streets of character that lent so much charm to Arbroath. It was demolished in the late 1960s to make way for the dual carriageway. The viewpoint is from the Millgate Loan end looking towards Ladyloan. The imposing building facing the camera was the original Station House of the Dundee and Arbroath Joint Railway, The crossing about half-way down is Hannah Street.

Left - A stained glass window to the memory of the members of the Arbroath lifeboat crew who lost their lives in the lifeboat disaster of October, 1953, was presented to St John's Methodist Church in February, 1955, by the widow and daughter of Coxswain David Bruce. The window was unveiled at a special service by the Rev Norman N. Faid. It was dedicated 'To the Glory of God and in memory of Coxswain David Bruce and members of his crew who perished in the Arbroath Lifeboat Disaster on 27th October, 1953'. Our picture, taken following the unveiling, shows the Rev Faid with Provost J.K. Moir and Lady Provost Mrs A.B. Mitchell and two RNLI officials, Commander R.A. Gould and a colleague.

Right - Nothing seen in the foreground of this picture taken from The Signal Tower in 1955 remains today. Most of the sturdy sandstone buildings were demolished to make way for Arbroath's inner relief road The yard in the foreground was that of British Road Services and had formerly been the haulage contractor's premises of the Stewart family. Beyond the grainstore, at the extreme left, is the old Ladyloan Church. Next to that is the opening of Bell Rock Lane, so called because the stones to build the lighthouse were prepared in that area. The tall building in the centre, originally the Dundee and Arbroath Joint Railway Hotel, was later divided into flats. The attic window seen towards the right hand edge of The Black Shed roof was that of the Gayfield Bar. The white building at the right was the premises of Thomson, McFarlane, Ltd., iron and steel merchants. Behind McFarlane's, the wooden building with the light coloured gable housed the generating equipment of what was initially the Arbroath Light and Power Co. Ltd., which, when the picture was taken, was the responsibility of the North of Scotland Hydro Electric Board. In the middle distance at left, the light coloured building and those adjoining formed 'Nicollie's Mill' and, just above that, may be discerned the Alma Works of Francis Webster and Sons, Ltd. The prominent chimney stack towards the right is that of the Arbroath Herald, Ltd., which was much reduced in height shortly afterwards and finally removed completely in the early 1980s.

The first boat to be launched from the local yard of Gerrard Brothers, boatbuilders, was AH 27, 'Bairn's Pride', built for David Swankie, 34 Union Street East. She took to the water from the yard adjacent to the lifeboat shed on April 7, 1955, in what was the first launch in the town for more than 50 years. Our picture shows the vessel, dressed overall in flags and bunting, being guided to the inner dock for fitting out.

Players of Dowrie FC pictured in 1955. They are, from left, back - Don Stirling, John Anderson, Robert Cameron, Bill Drummond, Ian Hosie and Jack (Sailor) Cargill: front - Dave Cameron, Frank Wallace, Jack Cameron, Sid Sherriffs and Colin Beattie.

Arbroath Town Mission Crusade Choir, which was formed by Town Missionary, Mr Bob Clapham, following the great crusade in Scotland in 1955 by American evangelist, Dr Billy Graham. The members are, from left, back row - Beryl Angus, Wilma Swankie, Andrew ------, Betty McLeod, --------, David Searle, Wendy Bell, Joy Cargill, David Grainger and Ann Rattray: middle row - Maureen Thomson, John Davies, Irene Crabb, John Searle, Ann McKee, Francis Gordon, Norma Bell, Paul Smith, Jean McIver and Alison McDonald: front row - Miriam Davies, Una Robertson, Derek Smith, Ann McLeod, Mr Clapham, Pat Scotland, Philip Swift, Irene Hayes and Lena Chapman.

The Ashdale FC team which won the tug o'war competition at the Extravaganza at Victoria Park in the summer of 1955. They are, from left - Bob Longmuir, Stewart Watt, Jim Smith, Bert Gordon, Chae Watt, Jim Kennedy, Bill Pearson, Ange Cargill and Bill Corns, trainer.

The wonderful summer of 1955 meant a busy year for those involved in the tourism industry in Arbroath, but local youngsters did not miss out and the dock gates was a popular meeting point for locals and visitors alike. Here we see a group of youngsters, some precariously perched on the edge of the quay, fishing for 'podlies'. They are, from left, standing - Chick Borland, --------, -------- and Allan Teviotdale: seated - Angus Boath, Dave Cargill, --------, Vic Boath, Chic Furye, Doug Falconer, James Spence and Ian Teviotdale.

Brothock Bridge as it was in the summer of 1955. Although our picture shows only the north-eastern corner of one of Arbroath's best-known landmarks, all of the buildings have disappeared except one. The central edifice was part of the Alma Mill, operated by Messrs Francis Webster and Sons, and the upstairs part was the spinning room. After lying unused for many years it was purchased by Messrs Clark, Oliver, Dewar and Webster, solicitors, and their new offices were built on the site. Round the corner, in Market Place, the only building to have remained virtually unchanged is the former Burgh Police Station, which now houses Arbroath Tourist Information Office. Behind, and beyond the spectacular £80,000 'Superloo', is the upstairs premises which formerly housed the Baptist Church and later a showroom for R.M. Meekison and Sons, painters, Market Place. The decorative cast-iron balustrade to Brothock Bridge itself was dispensed with when the bridge was rebuilt in 1963.

One of the delights of Arbroath's hugely popular Outdoor Bathing Pool was the midnight bathing sessions held during the summer season. They proved a Mecca for young people from Arbroath and the surrounding area as well as a cosmopolitan representation of those on holiday in the area. Our picture is from August, 1955, and proves that some hardy souls actually took the opportunity to have a midnight dook, for which a certificate was awarded.

When the Arbroath and Forfar Railway Company Limited finally expired on Saturday, December 3, 1955, its waygoing was marked by a mock funeral procession to Arbroath Railway Station where the coffin was carried on to the train by pallbearers. A single wreath of carnations, grown by the Burgh parks department, was placed at the front of the engine, No 46464, by Mr John Clyde (right), parks superintendent, who was suitably attired in lum hat and tails. He is seen with the fireman on the last trip, Mr John Sherret.

The Ladyloan station of the Dundee and Arbroath Railway was demolished in January, 1956. The building was then 118 years old. The station was closed when the railway was rerouted in 1846 and became the parish poorhouse. Later still it served as a school until the old Ladyloan School was built. Until 1955, it supplemented municipal housing.

Boys of the 2nd Arbroath Scouts cluster round the campfire in the Keptie Road huts early in 1956. They are, from left, back row - Colin McNab, Michael Davidson, Peem Adam, Joe ------, 'Baff', Anthony Shellard and Jack Campbell: middle row - Jim Millar, 'Bobo', Bill Adam, George McSkimming, Ed Maxwell, Leslie Potter and 'Sev': front row - Angus Ross, Ronald McLean, Alan McSkimming, Angus Anderson, Eric Cronshaw, Jim Fairweather and John Thornton.

Arbroath Amateur Dramatic Club presented three one-act plays in the Webster Theatre during the last weekend of January, 1956. One of these was 'The Dear Departed', the cast of which features in our picture. It was one of the Club's two entries in that year's SCDA Festival, which took place in Forfar. The players are, from left, back - Alice Glennie, Bill Watt and Arthur Kerr: front - Isobel Spink, Sheila Hepworth, and Arthur McConnell.

The ladies' chorus of Arbroath Amateur Operatic Society's presentation of 'Bless the Bride' which ran in the Webster Memorial Hall during the second week of February, 1956 comprised, from left, back row - Lisa Suttie, Evelyn Malcolm, Ala Rogers, Joan Mitchell, Helen Coulson, Joyce Duncan, Jessie Hogg, Margaret Moss, Isobel Cargill, J. Reid, Norma Hamilton and Grace Allan: middle row - Vera McLean, Belle Smith, Jessie Birse, Ruth Gordon, M. Deuchar and Audrey Gunn: front - Sheila Pert and M. Thomson.

The WVS Joan Club celebrated its third birthday with a party in the Assembly Hall of the Webster Theatre on February 15, 1956. Councillor Mrs J.C. Ross, president (centre), presided and the principal guest was Mrs Mijesinha, from Ceylon, who cut the birthday cake. Also seated at the top table are, from left - Miss J. Beatt, Arbroath WVS; Lady Provost Mrs A. B. Mitchell, Miss Mollison, Dundee district WVS; Mrs Rita Donald, Arbroath WVS; Mrs B. M. Henderson, chairman of the Old People's Welfare Committee; and Mrs G. M. Mollison.

Ashdale FC, one of Arbroath's Junior teams, pictured in 1956. They are, from left, back - Jim Cruickshank, George Cooper, Len Rogers, Eckie Annett, Stewart Watt, Bert (Waggie) Nicoll, Alex Petrie, Bill Jeffrey and Bill Corns, trainer: front - George Smith, Eck Paton, Stewart Birse, Ron Dewars and Doug Webster.

Primary seven pupils in Miss Kydd and Mr Bell's class at Hayshead School who took part in a concert at the end of the summer term in 1956. They are, from left, back row - James Middleton, Joyce Cant, David Gerrard, Brian Littlejohn, Elizabeth Rose, Ian Clark, Eric Cawthorne, Grant Anderson, Grant Nicoll, Raymond Swankie, George Watson, Alistair Fairweather: second row - Tommy Smith, --------, --------, --------, --------, --------, --------, --------, Wilma Fraser, Graeme Cant: third row - Sheila McLauchlan, Marjorie Rae, Brian Sutherland, Bobby Matthew, Nina Tosh, Linda Simpson: front - Barbra ------, Ann Findlay, Ann Spink, Norma Craig and Valerie Anderson.

The internationally renowned Arbroath sailmaking company, Messrs Francis Webster & Sons Ltd., achieved a major coup in the summer of 1956 when their sailcloth was chosen for the Mayflower II, a reconstruction of the original Mayflower which carried settlers from Plymouth to Massachusetts in 1620. Our picture shows Mr George H. Hitchen (centre) of Francis Webster talking to Commander H.E. Semple of the Gourock Ropework Co. Ltd., chosen to supply ropes for the ship, and Captain Alan Villier, commander of Mayflower II on her voyage across the Atlantic, at an exhibition at the Scottish Council offices in St James's, London, that September.

During the late 1950s, this 'trackless train', the Brighton Belle, was one of the attractions at Kerr's Miniature Railway. It ran along the promenade in the company of the buses and fire engine belonging to Mr Matthew Kerr, snr., who is seen in the driving seat. His son, Matt, recalls that the vehicle was a very smooth runner, with a centrifugal clutch, two-stroke petrol engine, and steering by joystick rather than a wheel! Starting the vehicle was by starting handle, and Mr Kerr recalls that it had a vicious kickback, putting carelessly deployed thumbs at risk of fracture. However, once started, the engine ran with a beautiful purr. The model was based on an American Santa Fe locomotive, and was superbly built by a well-known Brighton manufacturer and craftsman, Ernie Johnston. There was a plan to run it on rails instead of the road and bogies were designed, and built by Douglas Fraser & Sons, Ltd. but they were never fitted in Arbroath.

The picture was taken in Queen's Drive, at the rear of the Outdoor Bathing Pool.

Taken only a couple of years after the school opened, this picture shows primary three pupils at Hayshead Primary School in 1956. They are, from left, back row - David Patterson, Robert Reid, John Ford, Raymond Holt, David Phillips, Terry McCrodden, Billy Tosh, Andrew Spink, Gordon Midwinter, Ronald White, Hamish Pratt and Ian Smith: second row - Derek Davidson, Michael Kucharski, Moira McGregor, Yvonne Thoms, Betty Farquharson, Noela Spink, Christine Webster, Margaret Cargill, Christine Laing, James Addison and Alan Campbell: third row - Joyce Simpson, Joyce Thornton, Pat Dorward, Anne Muir, Phyllis Hood, Caroline Ronald, Adrianne Gilmore, Christine Ritchie, Lesley Boath, Sandra Curry, Marisza Burza, Mary Cherrington and Isobel Clapham: front row - --------, Alex Cowie, Campbell Dempster, Barry Campbell and Douglas Cant.

Prizewinners of Arbroath Rifle Club with their awards following the presentation ceremony in 1956. They are, from left, back - Susan Jolly, Jim Jolly, Jim Hudgston, --------: front - Dunc Robb, Vince Alexander, Peggy. Cameron, Jim ------, Mrs Innes, Bob Cameron, Helen Dear, Rita Jolly, George Birse, Fred Parker, Bob Grace, Ally Rintoul, Bob Innes and Bill Cowie.

Taken on November 4, 1956, at St Mary's Scottish Episcopal Church, Ponderlaw, our picture shows the first church parade of the new 6th Arbroath Company, Boys' Brigade. The salute is being taken by Rear Admiral Ham, of HMS Condor, with Canon Charles Copland. The 'front row,' whose faces are seen in full, comprises, from left - Roger Skelland, David Brown, Pat Anderson, David Thomson, Lance-Corporal ----, The Rev J.S. Douglas, officer in charge of the parade; and Lance-Corporal Ron Edgar. Also in the picture, in the centre of the row of boys behind, are Brian Vettese and Eric Fulton.

Principal players in Arbroath Amateur Operatic Society's production of 'Call Me Madam' which received an enthusiastic response from the Arbroath public when it opened in the Webster Hall in the first week of February, 1957. They are, from left, back - Drew Brown, William Jamieson, George Rodger, Wilfred Forrester, Wilson Robson, Christine Lamb, Jack Lamb, Ian Spalding, Cissie Fleming, Bert Adamson, Jack Laing, Jessie Hogg, Bobbie Mitchell, producer; and William Robertson, conductor: front - Rosa Appolinari, choreographer; Bob Cargill and Dick Manders.

Members of Arbroath Meat Traders' Association and guests at their dance in Hotel Seaforth in March, 1957. Pictured are, from left, back - -
-------, Mr R. McGregor, --------, Mr J. Ewart, --------. D.H. Robertson, Mrs J. Ewart, Mr J. Millar, --------, Mrs Millar, --------, Mr J. Campbell,
--------, Mrs Fallon, Jack Lamb, Mrs D. Christie, Mrs Hunter, Mr Fallon, Mr J. Ramsay, Mr Hunter, Mrs J. Ramsay, Mrs Quinn, Mr Quinn,
--------, Mrs Moffat, Mr Moffat, Mr Taplay and Mr J. Gibb: front - Mrs D. H. Robertson, George Ruxton, Mrs G. Ruxton, Mrs J. Campbell,
Mr A. Ritchie, Mrs A. Ritchie, Mr J. Barclay, Mrs J. Barclay, Mr A. Campbell, Mrs A. Campbell, Mrs A.I. Anderson and Mr A.I. Anderson.

ARBROATH FIRE BRIGADE

Opposite - Pupils of primaries one, two and three at St Thomas RC Primary School in 1957 pictured with their teachers. They are, from left, back row - Charles Webster, Joseph Traynor, Russell Pyott, Billy Orzel, Alan Gerrard, Jan Stapor, Catherine Nairn, --------, Lydia Syme, Rosemary Cargill, Marianne Edwards and Carol Swiercena: second row - David Sharp, Ian Robertson, Gary Pyott, Colleen Riley, Jonathan Syme and Peter Mylles: third row - Paul Rogers, Gary Cargill, Carla Dora, Jacqueline Black, -------, Mr Andrew Logue, head teacher; Miss Hart, Father Peter Kaye, Jennifer Melville, Helena Stapor, John Jackson, Elizabeth Webster and R a y m o n d McCormack: front row - Margaret Sim, Christine Sharp, Loraine Fitchet, Dale Smith, Anna Plawecki and John Orsi.

This photograph has two major elements of interest: the miniature fire engine, bought in 1957 by Kerr's Miniature Railway; and part of the frontage of Lamb's Garage, which stood at Gayfield before being demolished to make way for the dual carriageway. Behind the wheel of the fire engine is the young Matt Kerr, whose father founded the Miniature Railway. The engine itself is a one-third scale model of a Dennis Fairey Type III, which when full-sized were largely exported, but whose design was ideal to be scaled down. Three such fire engines were built by Ernest Johnstone of Brighton in 1951, under the works plate, 'Johnstone's Midgets'. Number two in the series ran at Sunderland from 1951 until 1956, when it was purchased by Matthew Kerr, Snr., who sent it back to Johnstone's for a complete overhaul. It arrived in Arbroath by rail in April, 1957, to work alongside the two miniature buses which carried countless thousands of young passengers over the years. The fire engine had a Villiers 197 c.c. two-stroke engine, which was replaced in 1981 by Olly McLaren, West Newgate Garage. In 1997 it receiving another replacement engine - astonishingly, a brand new one, fresh from its crate, air-cooled and with electric starter. The ladder on the engine was replaced by Ramsay Ladders, Forfar, who manufactured the scale model to its exact original design. Note the poster in Lambs' window, 'Win an Austin A35 for a shilling.'

Arbroath Town Officer Bill Fairweather heads the parade as elected members and officials leave the Old Parish Church after the annual Kirkin' o' the Council in May, 1957. The front row comprises, from left - Bailie D.A. Gardner, Provost J.K. Moir and Mr William Smith, Town Clerk, while the group following includes Bailie D.A.S. Smith, Hon. Treasurer R.R. Spink, Dean of Guild Adam Cargill, Councillors Mrs J.C. Ross, Barclay Ritchie, David Wilson, David Goodwillie, Frank W.A. Thornton, Edward Joss, Jack Lamb, Sam Bryce, and George Watson; Messrs Harold Farquhar, assistant town clerk; James Duff, town chamberlain; Douglas G. Arkle, sanitary inspector; George H. Rodger, burgh engineer; Bill Samson, architect and planning officer; John Clyde, parks superintendent; Dr Norman Setten, medical officer; and Miss Ann Scott, welfare officer.

The Arbroath Lads' Club under-14s team during season 1956/57. Pictured are, from left, back - Willie Robb, manager; Alec Milne, captain; Ian Matthews, Dave Brown, Arch Campbell, Brian Esplin and Ian Brown: front - Tom Cargill, Graham Cant, Billy Carnegie, Ally Law and Mike Fox.

Arbroath High School primary department first XI football team in 1957 comprised, from left, back - Ross Ruxton, James A. Cargill, Ian Snowdon, James Cargill, Brian Maitland and Michael Powalski: front - Eric Cronshaw, David Neave, Roland McLean, Angus Anderson and John Thornton.

Arbroath Town Councillors, burgh officials and guests at the annual water inspection at Glenogil in June, 1957. Pictured are, from left - James Duff, Town Chamberlain; Councillor George Watson, Jack Young, Councillor Sam Bryce, Norman Crawford, Librarian; Councillor Edward J. Joss, Quentin Clark, Councillor Jack W.R. Lamb, Councillor David Goodwillie, ex-Provost John F. Webster, Councillor Alex Keith, Sheriff Harold Ford, Harry C. Nicoll, assistant Town Chamberlain; Douglas G. Arkle, Sanitary Inspector; Provost J.K. Moir, Councillor Harry Farmer, Bailie David S. Smith, John G.H. Clyde, Parks Superintendent; Bailie James M. McBain, Harold Farquhar, assistant Town Clerk; Alex Mollison and George H. Rodger, Burgh Engineer.

Left - In July, 1957, while their film star mother, Deborah Kerr, was filming 'Bonjour Tristesse' in Paris, Melanie and Francesca Bartley holidayed in Monkbarns Hotel with their Arbroath-born nannie, Miss Nan Patterson, whose parents lived at Colvill Place. The children are pictured with Matt Kerr, principal of Kerr's Miniature Railway, West Links, having a closer than usual look at the locomotive 'Flying Scotsman'.

Right - A picture of a painting of a picturesque scene. Famous Scottish artist, J. McIntosh Patrick, visiting artist at Hospitalfield House in 1957, pictured on a glorious summer day painting in the farm steading. The buildings have been restored in The Steading housing development, except for the whitewashed cottages in the iddle distance, which were demolished. In October, 1965, Arbroath Town Council presented ex-Provost D.A. Gardner with his portrait in oils painted by J. McIntosh Patrick. He was also gifted a painting of the steading at Hospitalfield Farm by the same artist.

Members of the 3rd Arbroath Troop of Boy Scouts pictured at their annual camp on the Glentanar Estate near Aboyne, Deeside, in August, 1957. Pictured are, from left, standing - Tommy Sinclair, Donald Forbes, Ian Sievwright, -------- and Scoutmaster George Ramsay: kneeling - Ron Nicoll, Allan Robertson, Michael Ritchie, John Mathers, Bill Eaton and Grant Clark: seated - Stewart Moir, Derek Duncan, Jim Riddle, Derek Sievwright, Billy Cromar, Bob McPherson, Tom Mathieson, Dennis Arnot and Michael Sievwright.

Members of the Arbroath Red Cross unit photographed at their annual inspection in the Red Cross Hall in 1957. They are, from left, back row - --------, --------, Moira Chalmers, Dorothy Marr, Annie Cargill, Sylvia Cant and Margaret Brown: second row - Isabel Smith and Marjorie Waldie: third row - Linda-May Scott, Heather Wood, Margaret Thomson, Elizabeth Whyte, Elaine Cant, Margaret Philp, Mary Reith, Dorothy Taylor and Rosemary Cossans: fourth row - Margaret Reith, Maureen Dewars, Miss Violet Morrison, Cadet Officer, Unit 122; Lady Montgomery-Cunningham, Assistant County Director (Youth and Junior); Miss Jean Cuthill, Commandant, Angus 24 Volunteer Aid Detachment; Sheena Winton, Marlene Boag and Fiona Lawrence: kneeling - Margaret Reid, --------, ---- Crammond and Rebecca Wood.

At the beginning of October, 1957, singer Dorothy Squires and pianist, Russ Conway, took a break from their show in the Palace Theatre, Dundee, to visit Arbroath where they were shown round by publicity officer, Captain Denis Cooper, MBE. A highlight of their visit was the opportunity to purchase freshly made Smokies at the Fit o' the Toon and they are seen savouring Arbroath's delicacy.

Local police officers feature in this picture, which shows the retiral presentation to Sergeant David Stott, of the Arbroath Sub-division of Angus Constabulary at the beginning of October, 1957. He was gifted a bicycle on behalf of friends and colleagues by Superintendent Frank Crowe at a ceremony in the Police Station at the corner of Market Place and Gravesend, which now houses the Tourist Information Centre. Pictured are, from left - Constable Dave Smith, Constable Will Stewart, Inspector Alex Christie, Sergeant Alex Knight, Sergeant Stott, Inspector Jim Middleton, Sergeant Bill Cameron, Superintendent Crowe, Inspector Charlie Tevendale, Inspector Tom McMaster and Sergeant Ian McLean.

Young people - as usual - were in the majority when a prolonged frost ensured that the ice on Keptie Pond was strong enough to bear a person's weight in January, 1958. The iron hard slopes of Keptie Hill were ideal for sledging.

In March, 1958, the Rev. Richard Bishop, North Church, Dunfermline, was inducted to the charge of Inverbrothock Church in a ceremony performed by the Rev. George Gillon, Barry, moderator of Arbroath Presbytery. Lessons were read by the Rev. Archibald Russell, Abbey Church, the Presbytery clerk. Our picture shows a group of minister following the service. They are, from left, Rev John Reid, Knox's Church; Rev. Bishop, Rev. Russell, Rev Charles E. Duff, St Vigeans Church; Rev Gillon, Rev Kenneth Macmillan, Erskine/Princes Street Churches; and Rev. Frank Clark, Carnoustie.

A new bridge over the Brothock Burn at Danger Point was laid by crane during the first week of April, 1958. The buildings in the background are in Old Shorehead and include the building with the exterior stair where a lay preacher would give his sermon on Sundays. The tallest structure is the top floor of the Commercial Inn and the building behind the group of workmen is Arbroath Fishermen's Association's premises in Marketgate. The 40-year-old bridge was replaced in 1997.

Although the Windmill Hotel is no longer trading, the establishment boasted almost 50 years of tradition and service to the people of Arbroath and further afield. This proud group from April, 1958, exemplify the standard that made the Windmill one of the premier hotels in the area. Pictured after having set up the main dining room for a function are, from left, Jim Oswald, barman; Bob Bowman, proprietor; Frances Cuthill, Olga Moore, manageress; Pat Watt, Bill McKirty, chef; Helen Mitchell, Thelma ------ and a catering student from Ross Hall Catering College, Glasgow.

These pupils at Parkhouse-Abbey Primary School in 1958 proudly display the cardboard skyscrapers they built as part of a class project on the United States of America, intended to give them an insight into its history and architecture. The youngsters are, from left, back - Alastair Cameron, Robert McDonald, David Fairweather, George Campbell and Raymond Heenan: front - William Thompson, Robert Smith, Donald Gowans, Mark Sanderson (Mann), Stanley Davidson, Ian McMillan, Michael Heenan and Peter Norquay.

This happy group of youngsters enjoyed tea and buns in Mrs Grosset's Primary 5 room at Arbroath High School in June, 1958, as a reward for their fund-raising activities. The spread was provided by Mrs Greig, the local president of Dr Barnardo's Homes. The youngsters had all filled the little papier mache houses which provided essential funds for Dr Barnardo's children's homes, and had raised a total of £76. We name the children in rows from front to back, starting with the row nearest the far left wall - Wendy Dale, Nancy Goodwillie, Marjory Meikle and Leslie Rae: second row - Ethel Margaret Gilmour, Monica Page, Heather Chard, Sheila Johnstone and ---- : third row - Sandy Keith, ---- , Linda McGregor, Joan Masson, ---- , and Karlynn McIntosh: fourth row - Angus Anderson, Ian Booth, Claude Yule, Jeffrey Dugdale and Alastair McKay: fifth row - Bobby Buick.

In June, 1958, a weekend 'Jubileerama' was held at Keptie Pond by Arbroath and District Scouts to mark 50 years of Scouting in the area. The event was attended by over 100 boys from the four Arbroath Troops and the Leysmill Troop. On the first day of the two-day celebration, one of the activities on show was pioneering, when the Scouts built an aerial railway, a rope bridge to the island in the pond, ornamental gateways and a derrick for raising and lowering rafts, which they sailed on the pond. There was a campfire in the evening. Following inspection on the Sunday morning, a Scouts' Own Service was held at the campsite. In the afternoon, there were displays of Scouting activities, including axemanship, timbercraft, ropework, backwoods crafts, cooking and first aid. A guest of honour at the event was Provost D.A. Gardner, District Commissioner, who presented the Golden Arrow Award to the 1st Arbroath Troop. Our picture shows some of the boys on the rope walkway. They are from left - Alan Milne, Fergus Ellen, Donald McBean, Tony Bogulak, Angus Milne, Kenneth Cargill, John Mitchell, John Miller, John Strachan, Tom Mitchell, Ian Wright, Duncan Robb, Bill Craig, Brian Addison and Derek Law.

How it used to be at Arbroath Bathing Pool during the summer months. Arbroath publicity officer, Mr David Lever, in the midst of a record entry of 200 children for the five to 12 years class during the second Tuesday in July, 1958. The winner was ten-year-old Helen Cheyne, from Quest Quarter, Falkirk. On the same day, there were 70 entries for the under-fives competition, and 72 in the Junior Miss Arbroath contest. In the Miss Arbroath competition, 17-year-old Dorothy Ford, 31 Hayshead Road, was the winner from an entry of 23.

A peaceful summer scene in Ladyloan before town planners decided to do away with all the characterful houses and replace them with an 'internal relief road'. Taken in 1958, the picture shows groups picnicking on the grass and others enjoying themselves at the pitch and putt. From the same vantage point nowadays, all that would be seen would be the sewage pumping station and the dual carriageway.

The hairst - 1958 style! No combine harvesters in those days, at least not at East Seaton Farm. Creating stooks as the sheaves come off the binder are Jock Ure, Willie Lilley, Eric Reid, Chae Ford and Jim Findlay. On the Fordson Major tractors are Ian Rae and Jim Gilbert.

Pictured in the Windmill Hotel in 1958 are trophy winners at the annual smoker of Dowrie Sports and Social Club, for employees of the Dowrie works of William Briggs and Sons, Ltd. With their awards are, from left, back - Dave Russell, Harry Cant, Dave Balfour, Alex Cargill, Jim Black, works manager; Dave Bowman, Jim Mowatt, Colin Beattie and Wat Stewart: front - Bob Greenhill, Jackie Cameron, Jimmy Smith, Dave Duke and Dave Simpson.

In the foreground of this photograph from the Arbroath v Berwick Rangers match on Saturday, September 20, 1958, is the remains of the Gayfield stand which burned down in the early hours of the morning of Thursday, September 18. The conflagration completely destroyed the centre and most of the west wing of the structure, causing about £7,000 worth of damage. All the players' boots were lost in the blaze, as were five complete kits, stockings, jerseys, training kit and numerous footballs. One complete set of jerseys, shorts and stockings was saved - they were at the laundry! Lost in the fire were home team and visitors' dressing rooms, the boardroom, the ambulance room, the referees' room, the press box, the club doctor's treatment room, ambulance equipment and treatment equipment, such as sun lamps. The Arbroath Round Table commentary box and all its expensive broadcasting equipment were also destroyed as was Arbroath FC's photographic record of past achievements. The outbreak was attended by Arbroath Fire Brigade and Carnoustie Fire Brigade, but there was little they could do, as the stand was blazing furiously before they arrived. The Berwick match was, according to contemporary reports, a dreich affair which Arbroath won comfortably, 2-0.

This picture shows the final service of the disbanding Original Secession congregation - the last in Scotland - in their church at the corner of Hume Street and Maule Street on Sunday, November 9, 1958. Preacher for that historic occasion was the Rev Donald Cox. The church had been opened in June, 1888, and was eventually demolished in the late 1960s to make way for the dual carriageway.

In November, 1958, the annual Service of Remembrance, organised jointly by Arbroath Town Council and the Arbroath and district branch of the British Legion, was held in the Webster Memorial Hall. The guest speaker was Sir John Ure Primrose, a former Lord Provost of Perth. Afterwards, wreaths were laid at the War Memorial on the High Common, where our picture was taken. Those in the picture are, from left - Provost D.A. Gardner, Captain A.J.T. Roe, chief of staff, FORA; Captain G.W. Tanner, commanding officer, HMS Condor; and Brigadier J.A. Oliver.

Principals and employees of Gerrard Brothers, Boatbuilders, and their guests who attended the company's Christmas dinner and dance held in the North Sea Hotel in 1958. Pictured are, from left, back row - Nan Wyllie, Bill Rose, Bob Dunn, Dave Milne, Merry Coull, Clem Jolly, Greta Jolly, John McCrodden, Pat Cargill, Gordon McKellar, Pat Murray, Dave Reid, ----------, Alf Butchart, Jim Brown, Betty Brown, Mrs Greig, Dave Young, Helen Young, Sandra Coffin, Margaret Watson, Stewart Watson, Margaret Law and Joe Law: seated - Pat Dunn, May Milne, Babs Rose, Beatrice Gerrard, Andrew Gerrard, Isobel Nicoll, Jim Nicoll and Bill Greig: front - Tom Wyllie, Stan Morrison and Norman Spink.

Shortly before Christmas, 1958, boys of the 3rd Arbroath Cubs hosted a 'Mum and Me' night at the Keptie Road Scout headquarters. Akela at the time was Jean Clyde. Pictured at the event are, from left, back row - --------, Helen Robertson, -- Rosevear, --------, Margaret Murdoch, Agnes Murdoch, Ellen Cant and Mary Walker: middle row - Mabel Christie, Nan Bowman, Evelyn Ruark, Pam Cossans, Helen Bowman, Lindsay Robertson and -- Robertson: front row - Roy Walker, --------, Rodney Bowman, --------, Ian Robb, --------, Peter Cant, Graham Ruark, David Nicoll, Colin Rosevear, James Christie, --------, Gordon Robertson, Michael Cossans, George Murdoch, Neil Ritchie, Graham Bell, -------- and David Robertson.

A Sunday School party for youngsters of Abbey Parish Church held in the church hall in 1958. Pictured are, from left, back row - Kenneth Cameron, Jarvis Ruxton, Ian Shepherd, Maurice Pert, --------, Wallace McFarlane, Ian Whyte and Peter Boath: second row - Mr Alex Lowson, Elizabeth Kinnear, Maureen Low, Maureen Shepherd, Monica Page, Tom Walker, --------, --------, Jim Cant and Grace Allan: front row - Elsie Forsyth, Derek Lowson, Jean Mollison, Margaret Mollison, Sheena May Cant, Helen Smith, Wilma Shepherd, Linda McFarlane and Pamela Baird.

Principals and chorus members of the Abbey Theatre pantomime, 'Dick Whittington', which was presented in the Webster Theatre in December, 1958. In the group are, from left, back - Tommy Walker, Cyril Reid, Ian McDonald and Ian McLean; centre - Aileen Campbell, Jack Laing, Gwen Williams, David Pelling (The cat); Gordon Moir, Norma Hamilton, Arthur Kerr and Vera Geddes; front - Alice Glennie, Sandra Shepherd, Joan Hogben and Pat Hutchinson.

Arbroath High School FPs pictured early in 1959. They are, from left, back - Grant Hosie, Barry Patterson, John McMillan, Dougie Ford, Ian Shepherd and Ed Furye: front - Alastair McCallum, Bill Cowie, Andy Reid, Don Meekison and Ron Kidd.

This group of retained firefighters was photographed at the opening of the Ponderlaw Fire Station on Friday, March 20, 1959. The ceremony was conducted by Provost D.A. Gardner. They are, from left - David Smith, Maurice Rose, Bert Spence, Dave Hadden, Ivor Davidson and Station Officer William Massie. The are standing in front of a Commer pump escape vehicle, ETS 357.

In pursuit of approval of a plan to build a shed for his steam traction engine next to a bungalow he was having built in Viewfield Road, Mr Ian N. Fraser, 30 Ogilvy Place, in April, 1959, took his case to the Secretary of State after Arbroath Town Council had given consent for the bungalow but had refused permission for the shed. A two-day public inquiry was held during which evidence was heard by Sir Robert E. Russell, who eventually decided that the engine shed should be permitted. Our picture shows Sir Robert, with members of the legal teams including Mr Donald M. Ross, advocate, Edinburgh, who acted for Mr Fraser, and Arbroath Town Council's legal representative, Mr W.D. Smith, town clerk, the architect who designed the shed, Mr W.M. Wilson and, on the engine, Mr Fraser himself, during a demonstration in Ogilvy Place.

Officials and members of the committee of Arbroath Football Club attended a reception in the Town House at the beginning of May, 1959, after the club had regained its First Division status by virtue of a 6-0 victory over Hamilton and a 3-1 win over St Johnstone in the final two games of the season. The St Johnstone match, on a Wednesday, attracted the biggest crowd of the season for the already promoted Lichties - 5,229. Our picture shows Provost D.A. Gardner, a keen supporter himself, handing over a plaque bearing Arbroath's coat-of-arms to club chairman, Hugh S. Nelson. Pictured at the ceremony are, from left, back - --- Paton, George Potter, David Goodwillie, David D. Wilson, George Hardie, David Chapel, Chris Anderson, manager; and George Watson: front - Wilf Forrester, David McKechnie, Provost Gardner, Mr Nelson and William Smith, town clerk.

This picture takes us back to a field at Balcathie Farm where farm workers are seen thinning sugar beet - the traditional way - in 1959. The picture was taken by John Henderson, the farmer's son. Pictured are, from left, Charles Jorgensen, George Finlay, Ian Cummings, Jimmy Robbie, Tom Wilson, Edwin Johnston, Bob Boehm, a former German prisoner of war who elected to stay in Angus after the Second World War, Alistair Reid and James Milne.

Pictured with their silverware at the end of the 1959 season are officials and members of the under-16 and under-18 Arbroath Lads' Club teams. They are, from left, back row - Dave Easson, Jim McKenzie, Jim Goodfellow, president; Angus Marnie, Chic Spink and Jim Fairweather, coach: middle row - Ally Law, Willie Jarret, Sinclair Stewart, Jim Cargill, Dave Brown, Frank Murray, Archie Campbell, John Bekier, Ian Stirling and Hen Buchan: front row - Graham Cant, Jim Fairweather, Peter Seroczynski, Duncan Ferguson, Charlie Smith, Dave Ferguson, Sid Dick, Ron Ferrier, Willie Carnegie, Brian Jarret and Tom Cargill. The season, the under-18 team won the League Championship, the Supplementary Championship, the Maclay Cup and the Nelson Cup. The under-16s won the League Championship, the Supplementary Championship, the Renilson Cup and the Urquhart Cup.

The 1950s in particular heralded a proliferation in the number of amateur football teams in and around Arbroath. These young men, pictured at the start of the 1959/60 season are members of Inchcape Strollers. They are, from left, back - Dave Strachan, Donald Sutherland, Ron Kerr, Steve Myles, Clark Hayward and Bob Ross: front - Jim Swankie, -------, Gordon Lorimer, Ray Thomson and Dave Freeman.

This substantial group of characterful buildings were sacrificed on the altar of development to make way for the town's inappropriately named 'Inner Relief Road'. Our picture would have been taken from the corner of the inner-dock nearest the Shore houses and adjacent to the Linies. The Linies (for the benefit of our younger readers, the railway spur that ran from the railway yard behind the railway station, down to the harbour) were just off picture to the right, as was West Grimsby. The gap behind the lorry in the middle of the picture was the start of Dickfield Street, and the opening to the left of the lamp standard was Bell Rock Lane, a cul-de-sac. The warehouse building on the right, at the corner of West Grimsby and Ladyloan, was occupied by J. & W. Henderson, builders' merchants, whose main access was in West Grimsby. They also had depots in Aberdeen and Dundee. At the corner of Ladyloan and Dickfield Street was the popular hostelry, the Gayfield Bar and Lounge. The licensee in the early 1950s was John B. Mitchell, a former LNER dining car waiter, who was followed by James B. Stirling in the run up to closure. At the opposite corner is the building occupied by J. C. Grant & Son, grain merchant, at 19 Ladyloan, who also had premises in East Grimsby. The imposing building between the grain merchant's and Bell Rock Lane was the old Railway Hotel, which faced the original Dundee and Angus Railway station, on the opposite side of Ladyloan.

Some 14 years after the end of the Second World War, the concrete tank traps which had been sited at every location where it was thought possible for the Germans to affect an amphibious landing, were finally removed. Interested onlookers watch as a Briggs bulldozer clears them from the foreshore at the West Links in June, 1959.

The annual Air Day at HMS Condor was an occasion to be savoured in the years after the Second World War and 1959 was no exception. During the middle weekend of June, some 7,000 visited the base to watch a display by Royal Navy and Royal Air Force aircraft and to visit the many displays and exhibitions mounted in the hangars and outside. As the day was Her Majesty The Queen's official birthday, HMS Condor had the distinction of being chosen to parade the Queen's Colour, simultaneously with the Trooping ceremony in London. A 100-strong Royal Guard paraded before Admiral Sir Walter Couchman, Flag Officer Air (Home). Our picture shows spectators watching an Avro Shackleton, probably from RAF Kinloss, during a flypast.

The flying of the Stars and Stripes and the Union flag at the Guthrie Port workshops of Douglas Fraser & Sons Ltd. on August 13, 1959, was a symbolic gesture which marked the merger of the local company with the Giddings & Lewis Machine Tool Company of Fond du Lac, Wisconsin , USA. The new private company so formed was called Giddings & Lewis-Fraser Ltd. For many years it was the town's main employer and the works covered the area on which the Safeway supermarket now stands, with the foundry taking up the area from Stobcross to Lochlands Street. The only building left is Angus Council's Bruce House, in Wellgate.

This view of Victoria Park dates from 1959 and gives a good idea of popular family cars of that period. Starting from the car nearest the camera and working along those parked nose to kerb from right to left, they are - Wolseley 6/80 (or perhaps a Morris Oxford), Standard 8, Austin A90 (or A95) Westminster; Austin A40 van, Ford Anglia (nicknamed the 'sit up and beg'), Ford Anglia (earlier model), Volkswagen Beetle, Hillman Minx, Standard 8, Riley 1.5, Morris 8, Austin A35, Morris Minor convertible, Austin 16 (perhaps), Wolseley, Austin A35, Rover, Ford Anglia or Prefect, Ford Popular, Austin A40 Farina, Vauxhall Cresta, Austin A40 Somerset, Morris Oxford, Hillman Husky, Riley 1.5 and at the shelter, a Ford Consul Mark II. The car coming towards us along the road could be a Riley 1.5 or a Wolseley 1500. The scattered group on the right comprises, from left, Morris Oxford, perhaps a Vauxhall Ten-Four, Morris Minor, Hillman Californian, Hillman Minx and hiding in the background, another Californian.

Some weel kent and respected senior residents fae the Fit o' the Toon at a get-together in the British Sailors' Society hall, the Coastie, High Street, in possibly 1958 or 1959. Pictured are, from left, back row - Liz Beattie, Meg Cargill (Polar) and Mrs Sutherland: second row - Mary Ann Smith (Moudie), Will Sim, Betsy Sim, Duncan Cargill (Daw), Jean Cargill (Daw), Tam Cargill (Dorts), Ken Tosh, Councillor Adam Cargill (Big Adam), Mrs Lizzie Pert (Lizzie Cammily), Jess Beattie (Blues), Joe Spink, Rab Swankie (Ranter) and George Baird: front row - --------, Aggie Cargill (McQuoise), Joe Cuthill (Cutty), Jean Cuthill, Peter Pert, Leeb Ann Bruce, -------- and Isie Cargill.

During the winter of 1959/60 and following a heavy snowfall, this picture was taken from one of the windows of the 'Arbroath Herald' printing works of Brothock Bridge. At right (from foreground) are the shops of A. & J. Campbell, butchers; East Coast Enterprises, the Central Bar, and T. Brown and Sons, grain merchants. Shortly after this picture was taken, the Central Bar extended into Brown's premises when the business moved into the present shop at the foot of Abbey Path. On the left is the corner of the single storey units which at that time were occupied by Isabell Ferrier, hairdresser; David Gove, baker; and Pelling's Gift Shop. The Bank of Scotland, previously the British Linen Bank, dominates the scene.

At Christmas in 1959, Arbroath Amateur Dramatic Club presented a pantomime, 'Aladdin', in the Webster Hall. The cast comprised, from left, back - Tom Walker, who played Cop; Graham Stockham, as Widow Twanky; Angus Anderson, who was Wishee-Washee; David Kane, who played Prop; Arthur Kerr, the noble Emperor; Jack Laing, as Abanazar; and Judith Sanderson, as the Ghost: front - Marlene Findlay, who took the title role; Helen McDonald, as the Princess; Sheena Munro, who was Pekoe; Joyce Cant, as Nycee; Jennifer Graham, who was the Spirit of the Lamp; and Margaret Hainsworth, as Spirit of the Ring.